Ono-isms

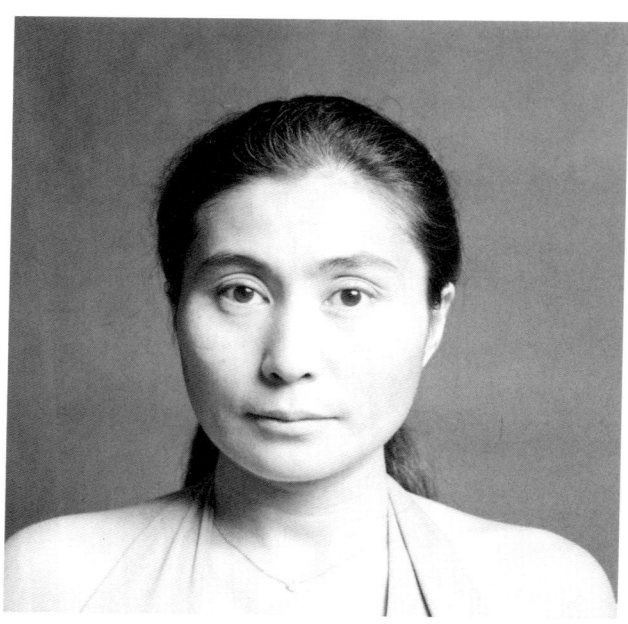

Ono-isms

Yoko Ono

Edited by Larry Warsh

PRINCETON UNIVERSITY PRESS
Princeton and Oxford

in association with
No More Rulers

Published by Princeton University Press,
41 William Street, Princeton, New Jersey 08540

In the United Kingdom: Princeton University Press,
99 Banbury Road, Oxford OX2 6JX
GPSR Authorized Representative: Easy Access System
Europe - Mustamäe tee 50, 10621 Tallinn, Estonia,
gpsr.requests@easproject.com

press.princeton.edu
in association with
No More Rulers
nomorerulers.com
ISMs is a trademark of No More Rulers, Inc.

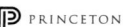 ℙ PRINCETON   ~~NO MORE RULERS~~ ®

Library of Congress Control Number: 2022945522
British Library Cataloging-in-Publication Data is available

This book has been composed in Joanna MT
Printed in China
1 3 5 7 9 10 8 6 4 2

CONTENTS

INTRODUCTION

In a career spanning more than seventy years, Yoko Ono has been acclaimed as an avant-garde artist, an innovative musician and composer, and a dedicated advocate for world peace. Her impact on global culture is remarkably diverse and far-reaching. Not only has she been celebrated in solo exhibitions at the Museum of Modern Art in New York, the Guggenheim Bilbao, Tate Modern in London, and other prestigious museums, she is the only artist of such stature who, as a musician, has had thirteen number-one hits on *Billboard*'s "Hot Dance Club Play" charts.

Ono was born in 1933 to a successful Tokyo banking family. Her education included a thorough grounding in music—one early lesson required her to convert everyday sounds into musical notations. In 1952, after two semesters at the prestigious Gakushūin University in Tokyo—where she'd been the first female student to study philosophy—Ono joined her parents in suburban New York, where they had moved for her father's banking work. Enrolling at Sarah Lawrence College in 1953, Ono spent much of her time in the music library, listening to radical composers like Arnold Schoenberg.[1] In 1956 she eloped with composer Toshi Ichiyanagi, a student at Juilliard, the renowned music school in New York City, and moved to Manhattan.

Ono's interest in avant-garde art and experimental music brought her into a creative circle that included iconic artist and architect Isamu Noguchi, influential composer John Cage, artist Allan Kaprow—who originated the performance art known as "happenings"—and composer and musician La Monte Young. In 1960, Ono and Young began presenting a series of concerts and performances in an industrial loft that she'd rented on Chambers Street in Lower Manhattan. In 1961, she had her first gallery show, followed by a concert of groundbreaking works at Carnegie Recital Hall.

In 1962, Ono returned to Tokyo for the first time in nearly ten years for a solo performance and exhibition at Sogetsu Art Center. She decided to remain in Japan for the next two and a half years, a pivotal period for the development of her ideas in art and music There, in 1964, she published *Grapefruit*, a collection of simple, poetic instructions for mainly imaginary acts. *Grapefruit* is an early example and cornerstone of conceptual art, which became foundational in Ono's work. That same year Ono first performed *Cut Piece*, a performance-art piece in which

Ono, dressed in her finest clothes and kneeling on stage, invited members of the audience to come on stage one by one and cut off part of her clothing. An intense experiment in audience participation and group psychology, *Cut Piece* is widely regarded as an early work of feminist art, and is one of Ono's most acclaimed works.

Later in 1964 Ono returned to New York and continued her work in events, film, and performance, including another show at Carnegie Recital Hall, *New Works of Yoko Ono*. In September 1966, Ono was invited by the *Destruction in Art Symposium* in London to lecture and perform. Finding new opportunities there, she remained and by November was having a solo gallery show.

Ono and John Lennon met in 1966, as the story goes, when he stopped by that London gallery show as it was about to open. To view her installation piece *Ceiling Painting*, Lennon climbed a ladder to the gallery ceiling, where he used a magnifying glass to see a message there in tiny print: "Yes." After two years of friendship, Ono and Lennon became a couple in 1968. Almost overnight, the avant-garde artist became an international celebrity.

Ono and Lennon decided to use the public spotlight to help promote peace and social change, including their 1969 Bed-ins for Peace and co-writing the songs "Give Peace a Chance" and "Imagine." At the same time, she continued to pursue her own music. Some of her solo albums of the early 1970s include *Yoko Ono / Plastic Ono Band* (1970), *Fly* (1971), and *Approximately Infinite Universe* (1973). After the birth of their son Sean Ono Lennon in 1975, Ono and Lennon made the decision to step back from public life. In 1980 they returned to the spotlight with the collaborative album *Double Fantasy*.

Immersing herself in music helped Ono emerge from the tragedy of Lennon's death that December, and in the decade that followed she created such notable recordings as *Season of Glass* and *It's All Right (I See Rainbows)*. Including the records made with Lennon, Ono has released more than twenty albums. The 1989 exhibition *Yoko Ono: Objects, Film* at the Whitney Museum of American Art marked a renewed interest in her art, which has continued to grow. While preserving and advancing Lennon's creative legacy, Ono's artistic trajectory has brought her increasing international recognition and acclaim.

Through her own words, this book offers a thoughtful and sustained engagement with Ono, in quotes collected from interviews, written works, and other primary sources. Reflecting her thoughts on art, creativity, social justice, and much more, these excerpts reveal, in Ono's

own distinctive voice, a complex, compelling.
and continually vital artist.

LARRY WARSH

1 Menand, Louis, "Yoko Ono's Art of Defiance,"
The New Yorker, June 13, 2022, https://www.newyorker
.com/magazine/2022/06/20/yoko-onos-art-of-defiance.

Ono-isms

Art

Art is the desire to be truthful. (10)

Art is not merely a duplication of life.
To assimilate art in life is different from
art duplicating life. (50)

I always believed that my work should
be unfinished in the sense that I encourage
people to add their creativity to it, either
conceptually or physically. (52)

Anything is art if you can influence people
by it. And if you can communicate
yourself with it. (19)

Art is my life and my life is art. (34)

————

"Idea" is what the artist gives, like a stone
thrown into the water for ripples to be made
(28)

————

As an artist, when you think about an idea,
you don't usually think about the risks
that it can represent. (12)

————

For an artist, everywhere is a studio. (7)

————

Anybody can be an artist. It doesn't involve having a talent. It involves only having a certain frame of mind, an attitude, determination, and imagination that springs naturally out of the necessity of the situation. (59)

———

You can become a stereotype of yourself. … This is what I really despise about the art world. You get a tiny idea like, "All right, I'm an artist who draws circles." You stick to that and it becomes your label. (26)

———

The role of good art is to instigate ideas in others. (131)

I don't believe in collectivism of art nor in having only one direction in anything. I think it is nice to return to having many different arts … just as having many flowers. In fact, we could have more arts "smell," "weight," "taste," "cry," "anger" … etc. (50)

———

By instructionalizing art, you did not have to stick to the two-dimensional or three-dimensional world. In your mind, you can be in touch with a six-dimensional world, if you wished. (7)

———

All artworks are conceptual. The part you see is only part of what it really is. (94)

———

Do what you can do to survive but never
compromise with your artwork. (79)

———

In the world of the artist, you give what you
have to society, but you're giving something
real so of course they're not going to take it.
That's normal so I wasn't fretting over it.
But it was a lonely trip. (34)

———

I was always avant-garde, even when
I was a little girl. (46)

———

In the conceptual world, [I] did not have to
think about how an idea could be realized
physically. I could be totally daring. (7)

———

I am not an entertainer. I am an artist.
You entertain people to give them joy.
You give art to people to chew on. (94)

———

Every person has their own opinion about
me and my work, and those are their ideas,
not mine. Once I've communicated
my art, I've done my part. (12)

———

To be an artist you need courage. (132)

———

People will understand my work, when my
work is necessary to them. (131)

———

People like Andy Warhol, who's a fantastic
original, beautiful artist ... added something
very important to the art world—or
the whole world—which is a
sense of humor. (4)

———

Art has an intrinsic value, totally aside
of its monetary value or the value of it
being exhibited in a certain way et cetera.
That intrinsic value is the thing that
is most important. (10)

———

Art to me is a way of showing people how
you can think. Some people think of art as
like beautiful wallpaper that you can sell,
but I have always thought that it is
to do with activism. (132)

———

Artists must not create more objects[;] the world is full of everything it needs. (59)

Creating is not the job of the artist. The job of the artist is to change the value of things. (131)

I knew that no matter how much you wanted, the work never stayed the same. So, as an artist, instead of trying to hold on to what was impossible to hold on to, I wanted to make "change" into a positive move: let the work grow by asking people to participate and add their efforts. (7)

Men can destroy/Women can create/
Artists revalue. (59)

———

I think that the power of art, music, and
films—anything to do with artistic, creative
events—can help to change this world. We're
trying to do it, and I think we will. (123)

———

I try to give only the illusion of destruction
in my work. (11)

———

So many people say, to me, "why don't you go back to 'performance art,'" as they call it. And I feel I never left. All the things I do now are part of that tradition. (66)

———

Art for me is like breathing. When I stop breathing, what happens? (36)

———

I don't particularly consider myself just an artist. I'm a woman—I'm a human be-ing—and there are a lot of situations that that covers. (20)

———

Art is a way of survival. (34)

———

Life

Don't think you have to balance life. Just enjoy life and life will balance itself. (98)

———

Life is like a suitcase[;] you can squeeze a lot in. (70)

———

If someone is unpleasant to you, draw a halo around his or her head in your mind. He/she is an angel who came to teach you something. (100)

———

We are all magnets. We attract what we need to attract to us. (96)

———

Every person's life can be a book thicker than
an encyclopedia and still you couldn't explain
all that they took to survive. (13)

———

Change is the nature of life. So enjoy
what it is now. (38)

———

All my life I felt like I was in the middle
of an ocean / Unable to touch the
horizon / All my life I was floating on
my emotion / Not knowing life had
its own motion. (117)

———

Everything you do in life is an event. (6)

———

The door doesn't open with the first knock.
Be patient. (102)

———

One cannot get rid of things by repressing.
In order to get "rid," you have to first "get."
(26)

———

If I get angry, I ask myself why I feel that
way. If I can find the source of my anger,
I can turn that negative energy into
something positive. (35)

———

We are all entertained to death. We don't have time to unfocus ourselves from the various daily entertainment we surround ourselves with. (79)

———

When are we going to lift our eyes and look beyond the screen? (124)

———

When you say search for self, you are searching for what you've lost because of all the other messages that are coming to you because of the hypnotism that you are put under by others in the world. It's as simple as that. (77)

———

Your room is an extension of your mind.
If a room is lopsided, just trying to keep a cup
on a table becomes a drama. If your mind is
lopsided, everything you do becomes a drama.

(109)

No power outside can destroy you. You can
destroy yourself by agreeing with them. (87)

I always think of myself as an outsider and
there's a power in that, there's wisdom that
you gain by being an outsider and that you
can bring into society. The main society
always benefits from what the outsider
can bring to them. (34)

Nobody can deter you, nobody can intimidate you, nobody can stop you, except yourself (87)

When you confront what you fear it disappears. (78)

Pessimism is not going to take you anywhere. (2)

Bless you for your anger / It's a sign of rising energy / (transform the energy to versatility and it will bring you prosperity). (29)

We were very wise when we were young.
We are getting a bit doubtful of ourselves
now. Don't be. The child in you
will save you. (103)

───────

Some people are old when they're 18 and
some people are young when they're 90.
You can't define people by whatever society
determines as their age. Time is a concept
that human beings created. (92)

───────

I've realized that shadows have no age,
race, or tears. (104)

───────

The past and the future and the present
are all sort of like one dimension, the same
dimension—it exists now. That's why now is
so rich, because it has the past and the present
and the future at the same time. (42)

———

I think that positive thinking is like breathing,
it's a necessity. If there is a gloomsday concept,
then certainly there should be a lot of positive
dreaming. We need that to create the
future for our children. (66)

———

We are not waiting for any moment, we are just living this moment as fully as we can. (10)

———

Some people say that I'm very optimistic. I'm not optimistic. I'm just practical. (32)

———

You say life is a bowl of cherries / You give me a bowl of pits / The pits will grow into trees one day / I'm getting my cherries anyway. (118)

———

I guess I'm just one of those people who, no matter what, could never have been comfortable with a mainstream kind of life. Yet all of us—every one of us, really—are looking for some kind of comfort level in our lives. And that level is not very easy to find. (14)

———

Next time you meet a "foreigner," remember it's only like a window with a little different shape to it and the person who's sitting inside is you. (13)

———

We don't want all of us to be the same.
It's very important not to break differences
but to break your idea of difference. We are all
in this together, as what we are. So we must
appreciate the differences. (7)

———

Walking on thin ice / I'm paying the price /
For throwing the dice in the air / Why must
we learn it the hard way / And play the
game of life with your heart. (113)

———

Philosophy is important for everybody. It is
how you choose to see the world. (12)

I started with racism and sexism in the
beginning and fought them so hard
and was finally ready to relax.
Then, here comes ageism. (86)

———

I don't really believe in the usual concept
of age. Let's say that it took me all this time
to be what I am now, which is a person
who, through a roller-coaster life, has
learned a few things. (41)

———

The kind of people who are going to be
attracted to me, are going to be attracted
to me whatever age I am. (44)

———

Let me be free. Let me be me! Don't make me old, with your thinking and words about how I should be. (63)

———

There was an incredible power that was against me. And that power, I hope I was able to use it to do something good. Power is power. It's energy. And if you get big, big energy, you can use that in a good way. (74)

———

Yes, I'm a witch / I'm a bitch / I don't care what you say / My voice is real / My voice speaks truth / I don't fit in your ways. (107)

———

If all those people hadn't bashed me, what would I be doing now? What I am now was made by all those terrible incidents. I thought it was terrible all those years, but when I think about it now, I realize it was a blessing. (31)

———

I'm always looking ahead, and if there is no possibility to look ahead, then I despise that situation. (20)

———

The desperation of life is really life itself, the core of life, what's really driving us forth. When you're really desperate it's phony to use descriptive and decorative adjectives to express yourself. (67)

———

Life is about focusing and balancing.
If you focus and lose your balance, you fall.
If you balance and lose your
focus, you die. (109)

———

I want to feel the truth by any possible
means. I want someone or something to
let me feel it. (56)

———

People need shadows to rest in. I would
advise you to send a bucket of shadow
to a friend. (99)

———

Somehow I always did what I loved to
do and did my best with it. I think it has to
do with being myself. Myself is not necessarily
a strong person or a brave person. I have a
lot of weakness myself, too. But I was not
particularly ashamed of that. (125)

———

We all do have some garbage in us and we
shouldn't be afraid of bringing it out, as long
as we end with a positive period. (26)

———

We have to learn how to turn around negative
energy into positive energy. (74)

———

Anything in excess is likely to be a sickness.
(95)

———

Giving gives you pleasure. Receiving can
be burdensome. (85)

———

In order to survive I try to keep on giving. (1)

———

The terrible thing about this society is that
money buys certain freedoms for you—that's
why people want money. Money is a concept
of freedom. You get your freedom ticket. (6)

———

I think it is nice to abandon what you have as much as possible, as many mental possessions as the physical ones, as they clutter your mind. It is nice to maintain poverty of environment, sound, thinking and belief. (50)

———

Love is our energy source, wisdom is our power source / Health is our nature resource / Growth is our future resource. (119)

———

It's very courageous to keep going. To say in spite of it all we had a good life. (26)

Each time we dare to do what we wanna do, we're living. (107)

———

Focus on the positive and help those things to grow. Stay well and healthy, and let's see what happens. (123)

———

I'm smiling to the future and the future's smiling back to me. (72)

———

Creativity

To create is to express life. (32)

———

Pushing boundaries is important in all my creative works. I think that is what artists do.
(42)

———

Don't be a slave to your old dreams. Just move on and see what dreams will come to you.
(101)

———

Do you know what your obstacle is? The thing you thought was an obstacle might be a great help. It's how you look at it. (105)

———

No one should encourage artists to pursue tragedy so that they might become a good artist. I wouldn't encourage that. You don't have to have tragedy to create. (48)

Think of everything that comes to you as a blessing and everybody that comes to you as an angel. Then figure out why they are. By doing that, you will not miss the positive opportunity which is being presented to you. (75)

Creativity is innate and it manifests itself in so many forms. It needs to come out somehow or it destroys you in some way. (106)

If you're criticized then you can use it
as an experience. Compliments, you
can't use. (20)

My whole life I have created things without
the consideration of how it's going to be
accepted, let alone if it will sell or not. (10)

I think if you have a persona you show the
world that's separate from your true personal-
ity, the strain becomes too much. What [John
and I] decided was just to be ourselves. We
didn't have a conference about it or anything.
It's just the most relaxing way to be. (66)

My career? I never think of it as a "career."
Art and music and all those things that I'm
creating are just part of me. (68)

———

When I get an idea, I choose the medium,
or should I say, the idea itself chooses
the medium. (122)

———

Most artists work in monologue form.
I don't believe in the artist deciding what has
aesthetic values, but in letting the painting or
music or whatever it is grow—be in a state
of process. Everything I do is unfinished, so
that you, or somebody else, add something
and then pass it on. (128)

———

I was a rebel even in the avant-garde.
They were becoming their own establishment,
another institution. I kind of rebelled
against it. (87)

———

Sometimes I have compared myself with
a scientist or something—when you discover
something and you don't expect the whole
world to understand it. I always thought
I was doing that kind of activity,
in art and in music. (40)

———

Composers spoke of me as a painter who was a dilettante in music. Artists spoke of me as a composer who dabbled in art. I finally said I was glad I was a dilettante whose ideas were not limited by "professionalism." (47)

———

I'm one of those people who can't do something unless I'm totally motivated. That's one of the reasons I jump from one media to another. (25)

———

Caution is like a disease, it kills ideas. Be daring. And caution will disappear. (61)

———

Most businessmen will take the safe route,
and if you're an artist you might say, this was
a hit in my past so we'll do the same thing
again. But we don't do it that way. That game
has no ending to it. What we do is dish out
what we have. The best of it. (95)

———

Each time we don't say what we
wanna say, we're dying. (107)

———

There is a kind of poverty where you have an
excess of things, and all your energy is
directed toward getting and keeping them. (53)

———

The maximum beauty can be ugly
to some people. (70)

———

There's no ownership in beauty. (81)

———

It's an illusion to think you're getting
somewhere. You're just wherever
you are. (84)

———

Reality can be elastic, and I want to see
how elastic it can be. (20)

———

Not doing is a lot of doing as well.
To decide that you don't put the finishing
touch to something might be a big
artistic decision. (95)

———

Everyone is an artist and a genius, I think.
If we don't choose to limit ourselves then we
are totally accomplished. I think people place
limitations on each other and on ourselves.
There is a great fear of expressing ourselves,
of making that creativity happen. (106)

———

You can be inspired by somebody throwing
something in a garbage can. You don't know
what's going to trigger your mind into
something beautiful. (127)

———

Experiencing sadness and anger can make you feel more creative, and by being creative, you can get beyond your pain or negativity. People's reactions to my work aren't necessarily important—it's fine if they have different opinions. If their response is good, then I feel good, but what I create has to do more with myself. When I express myself, I feel free. (25)

———

I think it is elitist to think that a trained movement is more acceptable than untrained and possibly unrehearsed movements. Dance is fun. (73)

———

If you want to do something good creatively, there's always gonna be somebody saying there's something wrong. (43)

———

I really like the idea of encouraging, inspiring people to be creative. Because we all have this creativity inside, but we're not always opening it up. It's an incredible pleasure to be able to interact with other artists. (123)

———

Creativity is part of the growth of human beings, just like creativity is part of the growth of nature. And whenever something stops your growth, that's when you really have to fight. It's very important that we keep creating things. (32)

———

I don't think of [creating] as talent necessarily. I think of it like a good radio. You can turn the channel and all sorts of things come. (77)

From the very beginning—very early in
my life—I kept telling all my friends about
the things that I found interesting. I felt I had
to tell the world about the things
that were going on. (12)

———

Don't be so concerned that you might
accumulate age and that might equal to not
being too good or not being too energetic as
you were. You become much more energetic
because you've accumulated wisdom
and experience and love. (42)

———

Our thoughts determine our age. (86)

———

Something that's very important for us to communicate is usually very simple. Like breathing: Breathing is very simple. You don't do a dissonant 9th harmony or something in breathing. You just breathe, you know? I think that's how it is with very important messages. (40)

———

Believe in yourself, and communicate your thoughts exactly in the way you think. That's the best you can give to the world. (79)

———

It's advisable to always keep your head empty so a wind can pass through. (99)

———

Nature and the Environment

You and I are the same element.
Only the container is different. (51)

———

Everything that is around us all has miracles
inside, if you just uncover them. (62)

———

There are so many of us in the world who
are now awakened, ready to act to save our
world. So, let's work together to save this
planet. Together. That's how we
will change the world. (37)

———

It is sad that the air is the only thing we share.
No matter how close we get to each other,
there is always air between us. It is also nice
that we share the air. No matter how far
apart we are, the air links us. (58)

———

The glass is actually 100 percent full: 50
percent with water and 50 percent with air.
(75)

———

The only thing that was permanent in
my life was the sky. (30)

———

All my life, I have been in love with the sky.
Even when everything was falling apart
around me, the sky was always
there for me. (109)

I am remembering that I don't just love
blue skies. I always loved grey skies as well.
To me, growing up is awakening to the beauty
of all people and all things in life.
And I'm still growing. (93)

I would like to see the Sky Machine on
every corner of the street instead of
the Coke machine. We need more
skies than Coke. (50)

Nature is the most beautiful music
we have on this planet. (76)

———

To me, there is something very wrong
about doing too much exercise while you rest
your other senses. I feel more human when
I'm just walking and wandering around
out in the world. (124)

———

Nobody's really alone. We all influence each
other ... The world is one big entity. (6)

———

Without the confusion and fear we would
see each other and ourselves clearly.
And without the fear, we would not
be afraid of being one. (106)

———

Instead of creating a skyline that challenges
the sky or something we should start to think
about the "earthline" in terms of being
comfortable and kind to the earth
and to ourselves. (9)

———

The value of gold can never be rated
as high as the value of water. (8)

———

I always felt the wisdom and love of water. (8)

———

This beautiful world of ours can still
survive and survive well, if we focus our
minds and actions on cleaning it up instead
of poisoning and destroying it further. (82)

———

Instead of thinking about doomsday all the time, think about how beautiful the world is. We're all together and together we're getting wiser. (97)

Let us wake up, come together, and work on cleaning and healing our planet, instead of further destroying it. Let's not waste one more day in creating a machinery of destruction. Give us a chance. On behalf of ourselves and all species on earth. We can do it. We must. (82)

My wish is that all of us will heal together and use the incredible power each one of us has. I really have incredible hope for the human race. (1)

I always felt that I had to give something
to the world. (126)

———

Our planet is full of beauty and joy.
Let's stay on it for the longest time. (124)

———

I dance to the wind, the sky, the sun.
We are children of nature. (38)

———

I have plenty of hope still. Large as
the Atlantic Ocean. (24)

———

Love

A drop of a genuine feeling goes a long way.
It's powerful, it's infectious, and it gives
a lot of energy to people. (47)

———

Love is the only thing that is going to
change the society. (5)

———

Love, once you have it, once you create a
kind of pathway for it to come out, it just
keeps on coming out. (71)

———

All we have to do is just admire each
other and love each other twenty-four hours
a day until we vanish. That's what we really
want to do. The rest is just foreplay
to get to that. (13)

———

You have to release your emotion in order
to keep your sanity. (20)

———

Each time we close our minds to how
we feel, we're dying. (107)

I can take hatred, because I don't believe that people are capable of real hate. We are too lonely for that. We vanish too quickly for that. Do you ever hate a cloud? (13)

———

Hate is just an awkward way of love. We spit on people when we want to kiss them. We hit them when we only want to be held. (13)

———

We're so ashamed of being jealous; so ashamed of being possessive. We're so afraid of having hate and all that. We shouldn't. It's all just different forms of energy. Energy goes through different forms. Nothing we possess is ugly. Everything that comes out of us is beautiful. (26)

———

The odds of not meeting in this life are so
great that every meeting is like a miracle. (13)

———

Bless you for the times you feel no love /
Open your heart to life anyway / In time
you will find love in you. (29)

———

I like the idea of everything being transient,
so that all that is with me is somebody
I love and myself. (53)

———

Love is when you understand it so well
that you finally relax. (17)

———

I never even thought of the word widow.
I thought I was a soldier. We were both
fighting for freedom and justice and
self-expression and [John] just fell
in the battlefield. (91)

———

I think that love will never die. Once you
know somebody, you can never unknow
that person. And knowing is loving. So you
can never get out of love. There might be
misunderstandings and separating for other
reasons, but love is always there. Staying
together is just one form of love. (26)

———

We can really have incredible, beautiful time together by loving each other, by being passionate about each other, instead of just being passionate about getting money and getting fame or whatever it is. I think that we should use our emotion in the most honest way, which is to communicate with each other. (42)

———

Whatever opinion you have, while we're busy discussing and arguing, our hearts beat in unison. This is a time to emphasize our unity and what we have in common. (95)

———

We have to strive to be real, that's all. Being
real is not something that just happens to you.
You have to sort of keep at it. (48)

———

Unless we teach each other what we really
feel / How are we gonna communicate
and get ourselves together? (111)

———

Each planet has its own orbit agenda.
Think of people close to you as planets.
Sometimes it's nice to just watch them
orbit and shine. (109)

———

Concentrate your mind on giving, loving, and thanking. Each time you give, you are in less pain. Give as much as you can. Find something you can love. Love as much as you can. Thank as much as you can. (55)

————

Each time you say I love you, you are actually sending love to the whole Universe and more. Our subconscious only knows that we are in a state of love that moment—not with whom. Let's stay in a state of love, and have lots of fun. (80)

————

Love makes everything work.
It makes everything grow. (26)

———

Remember you are loved. (29)

———

Love yourself for bravely sustaining
your life for so many years. (55)

———

Music

Music is like my security blanket. The first medium that I learned was music. (40)

———

Pop songs are a very strong form of communication. Most people think you write a pop song because it is a very commercial form and you can make more money for it. That's not it at all. Pop music is the people's form. (26)

———

The reason you create a new sound is because you're not that interested in the sounds that are around you. (69)

———

Once a song becomes a song, it has
its own fate. (48)

———

In my mind, sound and visual is all very
closely connected. It's mixed almost.
So when I hear sound, I almost hear
it in color as well. (48)

———

I've never seen a line between music and
art and performance. And that's a problem
for some people. (22)

———

Vocal expression has something so
directly connected to your body and your
mind. You're using your body and your
mind as opposed to a translator which is an
instrument. It's total giving, and it's
something you're giving on
a direct level. (78)

———

On stage, I think of me as presenting
this communication of gods and goddesses
within me—the real spirit and the real soul.
The cynicism that you have is not
your real soul. (34)

I don't believe communication is only on a conscious level. Even when you're asleep you can listen to a song and it'll enter you. Maybe it's better then because you don't have such conscious resistance. The lyrics can get into you consciously or unconsciously. (95)

———

Artists just creating a song and putting it down on plastic isn't enough in today's world. You have to communicate to get it around. (95)

———

My heroes were the twelve-tone composers— Schönberg, Berg, those people—and I was just fascinated with what they could do. (33)

———

Schoenberg, Webern, all their rhythm is ...
highly complicated and interesting, and our
minds are very much like that, but they
lost the heartbeat. (18)

———

All different musical forms are coming
together, now, and no one's surprised to see
a jazz sequence and rock chords in
the same song. (66)

———

Music is the beat of life for me. It's like my
heart. You have to keep on going. Motivation is
too light a word for it. It is life itself to me. It's
like I have to keep on breathing, it's a way of
survival, a way of being alive. (34)

———

I'm awkward in expressing my true feelings to people—whether it's to one, or the world. It comes easier for me when I do it in music. And that's how I do it. (77)

Dance music as a social phenomenon is very good because dance is healthy. (66)

[Dance music] is going to be known one day as high art. (36)

I get upset or excited about something,
and a song comes to my mind and I write
it down; it just comes to me. (39)

———

Somehow all the things that come out of
me—like words or music or whatever—seem
to be not my doing. It just comes in and
I immediately write it down, and I
catch it if I can. (77)

———

It is not possible to control a mind-time
with a stopwatch or a metronome. In the
mind-world, things spread out and
go beyond time. (50)

———

The only sound that exists to me is the sound of the mind. My works are only to induce music of the mind in people (50)

———

I have a very difficult time communicating my feelings; it chokes me up. It's easier for me to say it in songs or in artwork, or films, or performances. (14)

———

I used my voice to communicate in the way I thought was best. One has to use whatever one has, you know. (95)

———

[John's] guitar-playing ... was quite
avant-garde really, and we both suffered
because people didn't appreciate
what we were doing. (65)

———

My music is always trying to bring out
the truth in the world. (34)

———

Women in Society

We want justice, not equality. I myself
do not want to be equated with men, I want
to always be me. (89)

———

No woman ever went through penis envy.
We never did. The books say we're supposed
to, but look who wrote the books. (26)

———

I think that all women are witches, in
the sense that a witch is a magical being.
And a wizard, which is a male version
of a witch, is kind of revered, and people
respect wizards. But a witch, my god,
we have to burn them. (52)

———

You've got to show that women have guts too.
I mean whenever we sing something it's
always sort of Elizabethan poetry, pretty voice
kind of thing. I just wanted to show that we
have power. That's the aspect that's being
missed, that women do have power. (130)

———

We are in a serious identity crisis.
This society is driven by neurotic speed
and force accelerated by greed, and frustration
of not being able to live up to the image
of men and women we have created for
ourselves; the image has nothing to do
with the reality of people. (60)

———

I think we're all the same in a way.
It's just that society forces us into the
different roles. Men have to repress their
vulnerability and women have to
repress their strength. (95)

———

[A feminist is] anybody who's aware
of woman's struggle and what they have to
go through in the male society. (65)

———

Without men's cooperation in the end
[feminism is] not going to work. (65)

———

We must make more positive usage of
the feminine tendencies of the society which,
up to now, have been either suppressed or
dismissed as something harmful, impractical,
irrelevant and ultimately shameful. (60)

———

In the coming age of feminine society /
We'll regain our human dignity / We'll lay
some truth and clarity / And bring
back nature's beauty. (112)

———

We live in such a complicated age; we have to focus on uniting, we have to focus on peace. But it's easy to forget about the woman's condition. And the woman's condition is very bad. People assume we have equality when, if anything, there's a backlash going on against women. (22)

What most women were forced to be by social convention was to be slaves without financial independence. In a situation like that, was there anything other than *hope* we could rely on? (73)

Parents who raise children in modern
society unfortunately have great complexes
about women that they transmit to their
children. When I was a little girl my mother
told me that there was no female Beethoven.
I looked around and discovered that
she was right. There wasn't even a
great woman crook. (131)

———

Female lib is nice for Joan of Arc / But it's
a long, long way for Terry and Jill / Most of us
were taught not to shout our will / Few of us
are encouraged to get a job for skill / And all
of us live under the mercy of male society /
Thinking that their want is our need. (110)

———

We can evolve rather than revolt, come together, rather than claim independence, and feel rather than think. These are characteristics that are considered feminine; characteristics that men despise in women. But have men really done so well by avoiding the development of these characteristics within themselves? (60)

—

We are now at a stage where we are eager to compete with men on all levels. But women will inevitably arrive at the next stage, and realize the futility of trying to be like men. Women will realize themselves as they are, and not as beings comparative to or in response to men. As a result, the feminist revolution will take a more positive step in the society by offering a feminine direction. (60)

—

Equality under the law and equality in real life is slightly different. People are different from how the law can control them. We have a very complex life called the human life. There's more than equality in life. (90)

———

The ultimate goal of female liberation is not just to escape from male oppression. How about liberating ourselves from our various mind trips such as ignorance, greed, masochism, fear of God and social conventions? (60)

———

I think we don't have to do anything that we don't want to do. If there's a woman who prefers to stay at home and raise children and feels happy about that, she should do that. It's not *changing* the concept of our roles in the society but widening the *possibilities*. (95)

In a relationship I think women really have the inner wisdom and they're carrying that, while men have sort of the wisdom to cope with society, since they created it. (26)

You can't love someone unless you are in an equal position with them. A lot of women have to cling to men out of fear or insecurity, and that's not love. (3)

We were taught and educated to achieve
things or be something and, of course, doing
something in the house is achieving something, but people don't recognize that ... They
wouldn't believe [John] could simply—in
quotes—be a househusband. But at least
they asked him; they never asked me,
because, as a woman, I wasn't *supposed*
to be doing anything. (26)

———

The minute I was a widow, I started to
see what a test it is to be a widow
in this society. (74)

———

Childcare is the most important issue for the future of our generation. It is no longer a pleasure for the majority of men and women in our society, because the whole society is geared toward living up to a Hollywood-cum-Madison Avenue image of men and women, and a way of life that has nothing to do with childcare. (60)

———

The aim of the feminist movement should not just end with getting more jobs in the existing society, though we should definitely work on that as well. We have to keep on going until the whole of the female race is freed. (60)

———

What surprises me now is even though
discrimination against women and racial
discrimination still exist, they have improved
a lot, especially among artists. And just
when I felt I could finally take a break, I
encounter this age discrimination. (86)

———

If people looked at me as a feminist symbol,
I think I'd feel like a hypocrite. I'm not so
liberated; it's more like, I'm on my
way to, rather than, I am. (84)

———

There's nothing bad about feminism.
We have to help each other, because there's a
lot of women in the world who are suffering
because the fact is we're not equal. It's as plain
as that. It's still a men's world. (36)

———

Men and women are changing their
characters. Women are getting stronger
and men are becoming more kind and
sympathetic. It's been a BIG change
in my lifetime. (121)

———

I am proposing the feminization of society;
the use of feminine nature as a positive
force to change the world. (60)

———

Peace and Social Justice

It's time for action. Action is peace. (120)

———

You and I have the choice of changing
or not changing. (23)

———

I think the world is what we make of it,
and the world is a result of our dreams.
The dream makes the world. (72)

———

I'm not somebody who wants to burn the
Mona Lisa. That's the difference between
some revolutionaries and me. (57)

———

I don't think that revolution is necessary[;]
I prefer the word evolution. (89)

———

I believe in the mantra of the word "Peace."
People are like their language. (129)

———

We ourselves must be peaceful to get peace.
Once we follow that logic, and clear our
minds of anger, hatred, fear and violence,
we can see what we were doing wrong. (52)

———

We cannot enjoy the machoism of fighting
for peace. I felt that I wanted John's fans
to know that. You can stand for peace,
but not fight for it. (97)

———

Instead of changing the world, we should change our heads. That we can do. Our heads are on our shoulders not something that is in the horizon. (62)

———

The result is important, but so are the means. (97)

———

In order to survive and in order to change the world, first of all you have to take care of yourself. (26)

———

There are more people than politicians. Each one of us has the power to convince the world if we believe in ourselves. We'll make it. (54)

———

I'm all people who cry for their land / People
of the world walking hand in hand. (116)

———

Politicians rely on the fact that people
are not thinking. And if each person, all of
us, would really be centered and really start
thinking for ourselves, then they
don't have a chance. (5)

———

Instead of criticizing the people who are
being violent, who are in power, we need
to put ourselves in a position to create
our own power. (106)

———

I like to fight the establishment by using methods that are so far removed from the establishment-type thinking that the establishment doesn't know how to fight back. (59)

———

Indifference is the most poisonous thing. You can definitely deal with hate but not with indifference. (1)

———

We are getting wise on an individual level, so why don't we get wise about communication with the government? (16)

———

One danger that we get into, especially the liberals or hip people or whatever, is that they're so critical of each other or themselves that they can't unite. One thing that's important is to allow each other to use our own methods. People coming together who are so opinionated that they don't know what to do; that's the trap intellectuals fall into. We have to understand that we only have one heart each, one life each. (95)

———

Exorcise institution / Exercise intuition / Mobilize transition / With inspiration for life.

(115)

———

The wishes that we make, even if it's just written on paper and nobody sees it, I think they do affect the world and the universe. (9)

If the people in China can shift the axis of the globe by jumping at the same time, we can shift the axis of the world to Peace TOGETHER. Together is the key here. (79)

I think that peace marches are still very appropriate, so that all of us know that we're together. But I think that we have to find other ways of really being effective. (21)

Life is how we dance, not how we march.
(45)

———

Dream power / Dream reality /
Dream together. (114)

———

There are many people like me, who don't
want to give up life. ... We have to walk
this road of hope together. (32)

———

Believe in yourself and you will change
the world. (134)

People think of fantasy as different from
reality, but fantasy is almost like the reality
that will come. Everyone creates the fantasies,
so everyone creates the reality. (26)

———

We as the human race have a history of
losing our emotional equilibrium when we
discover different thought patterns in others.
Many wars have been fought as a result.
It's about time to recognize that it is
all right to be wearing different hats as
our heartbeat is always one. (83)

———

I feel that this world is extremely young.
We wanted to explore violence. The limits of
violence, how far we can go. It's almost like a
symbol of how much power we have. Violence
was a mystery that we wanted to explore.
Now we did to the point that we know
that the mystery's over. (72)

———

Society does not mature on its own.
We are the society. So we have to work to
bring true awareness to ourselves. (124)

———

I think violence is just a state of mind that
arises when you have a deep resentment at
not being able to communicate. (64)

———

Whatever opinion you have, while we're busy discussing and arguing, our hearts beat in unison. (95)

————

Anger just hurts yourself. (1)

————

You can assassinate a leader, but it's hard to assassinate two billion people. It's time for each one of us to take responsibility of being the one to do the right thing together.

(124)

————

Healing yourself is connected with healing others. Quite often it's not that easy to heal yourself, it's much easier to reach out and heal others and by doing that, you heal yourself. (34)

———

Find peace in your heart and it will spread over the world. The effect of it is strong and immediate. Keep your quiet center, and stand for peace, instead of fighting for peace. We can do it. (15)

———

You can eat meditating, you can walk meditating. Meditation is the culture of peace. And so when you're creating a life of meditation, then you're actually directly connecting yourself with world peace. Keep on living a life of meditation, and let's all achieve world peace through that. (88)

———

If we each contribute one thing a day then we'll have the future that we want. It doesn't have to be waving a flag. It could just be opening one part of your mind, secretly. (95)

———

Once we change our heads, we will see that the world peace will reign on us without us even lifting our fingers. (62)

———

There are only two classes left in our society. The class who communicates and the class who doesn't. Tomorrow I hope there will be just one. Total communication equals peace. (59)

—————

We talk about having a belief in youth, but youth includes everybody that is youthful, naturally. (27)

—————

I think most people are activists now—it's a very beautiful age, when we're starting to become more aware that we have to work together to make things better. (35)

—————

All of us are part of the future. The future
is already within us. (26)

———

Have courage, have rage, we're rising. (108)

———

Shed light, and darkness disappears. (133)

———

They say that the fight at dawn is the
severest and I think this is the time of dawn.
In other words, I think it's going to be
better very soon. (23)

———

Listen to your heart / Respect your intuition /
Make your manifestation / There's no
limitation / Have courage / Have rage /
We're all together. (108)

———

A dream you dream alone is only a dream,
a dream you dream together is reality. (49)

———

Think Peace. Act Peace. Spread Peace.
Imagine Peace. (120)

———

SOURCES

Some quotes have been lightly edited for clarity

1. Cott, Jonathan. *Days That I'll Remember: Spending Time with John Lennon and Yoko Ono.* New York: Doubleday, 2013.

2. Ono, Yoko. Interview by Howard Smith. Mississuaga, Ontario, December 17, 1969. WABC. Broadcast December 1969.

3. Ono, Yoko. Interview by Tariq Ali and Robin Blackburn. January 21, 1971. http://www.beatlesinterviews.org /db1971.0121.beatles.html

4. Ono, Yoko. *The Dick Cavett Show.* Interview by Dick Cavett. ABC. Recorded September 8, 1971. Broadcast September 24, 1971.

5. Ono, Yoko. Interview by Dave Sholin and Laurie Kaye. RKO. Recorded December 8, 1980. Partially broadcast December 14, 1980.

6. Lennon, John, and Yoko Ono. Bed-in Press Conference, Amsterdam, 1969. In *The Lost Lennon Interviews,* edited by Laura Morin. Holbroook: Adams Media Corporation, 1996.

7. Ono, Yoko, and Hans Ulrich Obrist. "Mix a Building and the Wind, New York, November 2001." In *Yoko Ono—Hans Ulrich Obrist: The Conversation Series,* edited by Hans Ulrich Obrist, 7–32. Köln: König, 2009.

8. Ono, Yoko, and Hans Ulrich Obrist. "Questions for *Water Event, Oslo, February 2005.*" In *Yoko Ono—Hans Ulrich Obrist: The Conversation Series*, edited by Hans Ulrich Obrist, 33–38. Köln: König, 2009.

9. Ono, Yoko, and Hans Ulrich Obrist. "The Architecture Interview, Van Alen Institute, New York, June 2008." In *Yoko Ono—Hans Ulrich Obrist: The Conversation Series*, edited by Hans Ulrich Obrist, 39–62. Köln: König, 2009.

10. Ono, Yoko, and Hans Ulrich Obrist. "Artistic Freedom, Inspiration and Space Transformers, Telephone Interview, April 2009." In *Yoko Ono—Hans Ulrich Obrist: The Conversation Series*, edited by Hans Ulrich Obrist, 63–76. Köln: König, 2009.

11. Ono, Yoko, and Hans Ulrich Obrist. "Early Morning: A Conversation with Gustav Metzger, London, June 2009." In *Yoko Ono—Hans Ulrich Obrist: The Conversation Series*, edited by Hans Ulrich Obrist, 77–91. Köln: König, 2009.

12. Ono, Yoko, and Hugo Huerta Marin. "Yoko Ono." In *Portrait of an Artist: Conversations with Trailblazing Creative Women*, edited by Hugo Huerta Marin, 136–49. Munich: Prestel, 2021.

13. Ono, Yoko. "Feeling the Space." *New York Times*, August 24, 1973.

14. Kemp, Mark. "Yoko Ono Reconsidered." *Option*, July 1992. https://www.rocksbackpages.com/Library/Article/yoko-ono-reconsidered.

15. Ono, Yoko. "Give Peace a Chance." Speech at Oxford University, October 2002.
16. Ono, Yoko. Interview, *New York*, January 1983.
17. Ono, Yoko. Interview by Hilary Henson. *Women's Hour.* BBC radio, May 28, 1971.
18. Wenner, Jann S. *Lennon Remembers.* London: Verso, 2000.
19. Ono, Yoko. *This Is Not Here* exhibition press conference, Everson Museum, Syracuse, October 8, 1971.
20. Mitchell, Elvis. "Yoko Ono." *Interview*, November 26, 2013. https://www.interviewmagazine.com/culture/yoko-ono-1.
21. Tamarkin, Jeff. "Yoko Ono: A 'Lost' Interview, From the Dakota." *Best Classic Bands*, 2003. https://bestclassicbands .com/yoko-ono-interview-2003-2-18-177/.
22. Brady, Tara. "Happy Birthday Yoko Ono: Revisiting a Classic Interview." *Hot Press*, February 18, 2021. https://www .hotpress.com/music/happy-birthday-yoko-ono-revisiting -a-classic-interview-2-22892660.
23. Coney, Brian. "Yoko Ono—'It seems like plain hypocrisy that I'm alive, surviving and not speaking out.'" *Loud and Quiet*, October 18, 2018. https://www.loudandquiet.com /interview/yoko-ono-it-seems-like-plain-hypocrisy-that -im-alive-surviving-and-not-speaking-out/.
24. Aubrey, Elizabeth. "The Big Read—Yoko Ono: Imagine the Future." NME, December 27, 2018. https://www .nme.com/big-reads/yoko-ono-interview-imagine-big -read-2423954.

25. MacDonald, Scott. "Yoko Ono: Ideas on Film." *Film Quarterly* 43, no. 1 (1989): 2–23. https://womenfilmeditors.princeton.edu/assets/pdfs/ONO_Ideas_on_Film_MacDonald.pdf.

26. Sheff, David. *All We Are Saying: The Last Major Interview with John Lennon and Yoko Ono.* New York: St. Martin's, 2001.

27. Lennon, John, and Yoko Ono. Toronto Peace Conference, December 1969.

28. Monroe, Alexandra. "Spirit of YES: The Art and Life of Yoko Ono." In *YES Yoko Ono*, edited by Alexandra Monroe with Jon Hendricks, 10–37. New York: Japan Society and Harry N. Abrams, 2000.

29. Ono, Yoko, composer/vocalist. "Revelations." Released November 7, 1995. Track 13 on *Rising*. Capitol / EMI Records, CD. © Ono Music administered by Downtown Music Publishing.

30. Cohen, Brigid. "Limits of National History: Yoko Ono, Stefan Wolpe, and Dilemmas of Cosmopolitanism." *Musical Quarterly* 97, no. 2 (2014): 181–237.

31. Myskow, Nina. "Yoko Ono: I'm 80, I'm a Control freak and I'm Going for It." *Times*, October 22, 2013. https://www.thetimes.co.uk/article/yoko-ono-im-80-im-a-control-freak-and-im-going-for-it-9n7qfglqr2t.

32. Jardin, Xeni. "Interview: Yoko Ono." *Boing Boing*, August 6, 2011. https://boingboing.net/2011/08/06/yoko.html.

33. Gomez, Edward M. "Music of the Mind from the Voice of Raw Soul" In YES Yoko Ono, edited by Alexandra Monroe with Jon Hendricks, 230–237. New York: Japan Society and Harry N. Abrams, 2000.

34. True, Everett. "A Conversation with Yoko Ono." *Careless Talk Costs Lives*, no. 11 (2002). Full transcript published on *Collapse Board*, November 4, 2011. https://collapseboard.com/a-conversation-with-yoko-ono/.

35. Ono, Yoko, as told to Stephanie Palumbo. "5 Things Yoko Ono Knows for Sure." *O: The Oprah Magazine*, June 2012 https://www.oprah.com/spirit/yoko-ono-interview-yoko-ono-quotes.

36. Vollmer, Deenah. "Yoko Ono on Lennon, Love, Feminism, and Japan." *Interview*, March 22, 2011. https://www.interviewmagazine.com/music/sxsw-music-yoko-ono.

37. Holmes, Helen. "Yoko Ono Debuts 'I Love You Earth' Billboards with Serpentine Galleries for Earth Day." *Observer*, April 22, 2021. https://observer.com/2021/04/yoko-ono-debuts-i-love-earth-billboards-for-earth-day/.

38. Ono, Yoko. "Letter to Jane: Interview with Yoko Ono." May 20, 2010. https://www.imaginepeace.com/archives/11265.

39. Hammer, Max. "Yoko Ono Talks to IRC About Her Dance Hits, Collaborations, Sean and John Lennon, and Her Childhood." *Indie Rock Café*, April 18, 2010. https://indierockcafe.com/2010/04/yoko-ono-talks-to-irc

-about-her-dance-hits-musical-collaborations-sean-and
-john-lennon-and-her-childhood/.

40. Battaglia, Andy. "Yoko Ono." *A.V. Club*, October 16, 2009. https://www.avclub.com/yoko-ono-1798218220.

41. De Faria, Mitch. "Yoko Ono: The Lowdown—Sit Down Interview with Yoko." *Riot*, January 10, 2010. https://riot.nyc/yoko-ono-lowdown-interview/.

42. Harper, Simon. "In Conversation: Yoko Ono." *Clash*, September 10, 2013. https://www.clashmusic.com/features/in-conversation-yoko-ono.

43. Harper, Simon. "Yoko Ono Interview." *Clash*, November 11, 2009. https://www.clashmusic.com/features/yoko-ono-interview.

44. Coon, Caroline. "Yoko Ono: The Whole World Is My Mother-in-Law." Unpublished interview, 1974. *Rock's Backpages*. https://www.rocksbackpages.com/Library/Article/yoko-ono-the-whole-world-is-my-mother-in-law.

45. Ono, Yoko, and Ron Slomowicz. "Yoko Ono: About.com Interview." August 28, 2008.

46. Allen, Jim. "Interview with Yoko Ono." *Prefix Magazine*, July 10, 2008.

47. Bracewell, Michael. "Rising Sun: Interview with Yoko Ono, Frieze 64." January–February 2002. http://www.frieze.com/issue/article/rising_sun/.

48. Zollo, Paul. "A Conversation with Yoko, Part Two." *American Songwriter*, 1992. https://americansongwriter.com/yoko-ono-part-two/.

49. Ono, Yoko. *Grapefruit*. Tokyo: Wunternaum Press, 1964. 4th ed. New York: Simon & Schuster, 2000.

50. Ono, Yoko. "To the Wesleyan People." Lecture delivered at Wesleyan University, Middletown, CT, January 1965.

51. Robecchi, Michele. "My Mummy Was Beautiful." *Contemporary Magazine*, no. 84, 2006.

52. Richardson, Mark. "Yoko Ono." Pitchfork, February 12, 2007. https://pitchfork.com/features/interview/6541-yoko-ono/.

53. Hertzberg, Hendrik. "John and Yoko Take Manhattan." *New Yorker*, January 1, 1972. https://www.newyorker.com/magazine/1972/01/08/everywheres-somewhere.

54. Ono, Yoko. Facebook and Twitter Q&A. September 5, 2014.

55. Ono, Yoko. Facebook and Twitter Q&A. September 12, 2014.

56. Ono, Yoko. "Words of a Fabricator." Originally published in *SAC Journal*, no. 24, (May 1962), Tokyo. Translated by the artist, August 26–27, 1999. In *Yoko Ono: One Woman Show, 1960–1971*, 114–15. New York: Museum of Modern Art, 2015.

57. Smith, Alan. "I Don't Like All This Dribblin' Pop-opera-jazz. I Like POP Records." *Hit Parader*, February 1972.

58. Ono, Yoko. "Notes on the Lisson Gallery Show." Originally published in *Yoko Ono Half-a-Wind Show*, exhibition catalogue. London: Lisson Gallery, 1967. In *Yoko Ono: One*

Woman Show, 1960–1971, edited by Kyle Bentley, 180–181. New York: Museum of Modern Art, 2015.

59. Ono, Yoko. "What Is the Relationship Between the World and the Artist?" May, 1971.

60. Ono, Yoko. "The Feminization of Our Society," 1971. In *Yoko Ono: One Woman Show, 1960–1971*, edited by Kyle Bentley, 217–18. New York: Museum of Modern Art, 2015.

61. Ono, Yoko. Facebook and Twitter Q&A. July 25, 2015.

62. Ono, Yoko. "Uncover," essay written in Tokyo, Japan, July 23, 2014. First published at https://www.imaginepeace.com/archives/20557.

63. Ono, Yoko. "Don't Stop Me!" writing, February 18, 2015. First published at https://www.imaginepeace.com/archives/21173.

64. Mandelkau, Jamie, and William Bloom. "Interview Piece: Yoko Ono and Grapefruit." *International Times* 1, no. 110 (1971): 11, 15, 20.

65. Interview with John and Yoko, BBC Radio, 1980.

66. Rowland, Mark. "Yoko Ono's Sweet Vindication." *Musician*, December 1984. https://www.rocksbackpages.com/Library/Article/yoko-onos-sweet-vindication.

67. Cott, Jonathan. "Yoko Ono and Her Sixteen-Track Voice." *Rolling Stone*, March 18, 1971. https://www.rollingstone.com/music/music-news/yoko-ono-and-her-sixteen-track-voice-237782/.

68. Rothman, Lily. "10 Questions for Yoko Ono." *Time*, Septem-

ber 16, 2013. https://content.time.com/time/subscriber /article/0,33009,2151142,00.html.

69. Babcock, Jay. "Scream at the Sky: Thurston Moore and Byron Coley Talk with Yoko Ono." *Arthur*, October 1, 2007. https://arthurmag.com/2007/10/01/yokoono/.

70. Petridis, Alexis. "Yoko Ono: 'I thought my music was beautiful all along.'" *Guardian*, February 22, 2016. https:// www.theguardian.com/music/2016/feb/22/yoko-ono -interview-i-thought-my-music-was-beautiful-all-along.

71. Davis, Petra. "Every Day Counts: Yoko Ono Interviewed." *The Quietus*, October 16, 2013. https://thequietus.com /articles/13620-yoko-ono-interview.

72. Fass, Bob, and Cathie Revland. "Interview: Yoko Ono." *High Times*, no. 93, May 1983.

73. Shepherd, Julianne Escobedo. "Walking on Thin Ice: A Career-Spanning Conversation with Yoko Ono." *Spin*, November 6, 2013. https://www.spin.com/2013/11 /yoko-ono-take-me-to-the-land-of-hell-interview/.

74. Junod, Tom. "Yoko Ono: What I've Learned." *Esquire*, December 8, 2010. https://www.esquire.com /entertainment/interviews/a9051/yoko-ono-quotes -0111/.

75. Ono, Yoko. "Game Is Not Over." Address presented at the Oxford Union, June 15, 2005. https://www.imagine peace.com/archives/2619.

76. Ono, Yoko. Facebook and Twitter Q&A. October 18 2013.

77. Ono, Yoko. "Interview with Yoko Ono." In *The Guests Go in to Supper*, edited by Melody Sumner Carnahan, Kathleen Burch, and Michael Sumner. Oakland, CA: Burning Books, 1986.

78. Rothbart, Daniel. NY *Arts*, June 2002.

79. Ono, Yoko. "Femail." Excerpts from Yoko's fan mail replies, January–February 2008. https://www.imaginepeace.com /archives/2580.

80. Ono, Yoko. "State of Love," January 2008. https://www .imaginepeace.com/archives/2609

81. Ono, Yoko. "How to Fly." In *Museum of Modern (F)art*, December 1971.

82. Ono, Yoko. "As a Child of Asia." Address presented at the United Nations, May 4, 2005.

83. Ono, Yoko. "Surrender to Peace." Full-page ad in the *New York Times*, December 25, 1982.

84. Marsh, Dave. "Yoko Ono: Going It Alone." *Newsday*, October 28, 1973. https://www.rocksbackpages.com /Library/Article/yoko-ono-going-it-alone.

85. Greenstreet, Rosanna. "Q&A: Yoko Ono." *Guardian*, December 20, 2014. https://www.theguardian.com /lifeandstyle/2014/dec/20/yoko-ono-interview.

86. Murakami, Takashi. "Yoko Ono." *Interview*, May 27, 2009. https://www.interviewmagazine.com/art/yoko-ono-2.

87. Masaoka, Miya. "Unfinished Music: An Interview with Yoko Ono." *San Francisco Bay Guardian*, August 27, 1997. http://miyamasaoka.com/writings-by-miya-masaoka /1997/unfinished-music/.

88. Clerk, Carol. "Yoko Oh Yes! Ms Ono Speaks about Peace, Pop and Computer Games." *The Quietus*, September 24, 2009. https://thequietus.com/articles/02315-yoko-ono -interview-about-solo-album-john-lennon-and-the -beatles-rock-band-game.

89. Smith, Courtney E. "Yoko Ono Reimagines 'Woman Power' and Female Liberation, 45 Years Later." *Refinery29*, August 22, 2018. https://www.refinery29.com/en-gb /2018/08/208052/yoko-ono-woman-power-video -premiere-feminist-revolution.

90. Teeman, Tim. "Yoko Ono: I Still Fear John s Killer." *Daily Beast*, October 13, 2015. https://www.thedailybeast.com /yoko-ono-i-still-fear-johns-killer.

91. O'Hagan, Sean. "Yoko Ono at 80: 'I Feel that I Am Start- ing a New Life, a Second Life.'" *Guardian*, May 25, 2013. https://www.theguardian.com/culture/2013/may/26 /yoko-ono-80-meltdown-john-lennon.

92. Needham, Alex. "From Yoko Ono to Leonard Cohen—the Old Masters Finding New Inspiration." *Guardian*, February 10, 2012.

93. Ono, Yoko. Facebook and Twitter Q&A. June 19, 2015.

94. Ono, Yoko. Facebook and Twitter Q&A. March 20, 2015.

95. Cook, Richard. "Yoko Ono: We Are Only One." *New Musical Express*, February 11, 1984. https://www.rocksbackpages .com/Library/Article/yoko-ono-we-are-only-one.

96. Ono, Yoko. Facebook and Twitter Q&A. May 17, 2013.

97. Smith, Andrew. "Just imagine: Yoko Ono." *The Observer*, November 4, 2001. https://www.rocksbackpages.com /Library/Article/just-imagine-yoko-ono.

98. Ono, Yoko. Facebook and Twitter Q&A. September 5, 2014.

99. Ono, Yoko. "On Rooms and Footsteps," 1971.

100. Ono, Yoko. Facebook and Twitter Q&A. March 20, 2012.

101. Ono, Yoko. Facebook and Twitter Q&A. October 3, 2014.

102. Ono, Yoko. Facebook and Twitter Q&A. September 19, 2014.

103. Ono, Yoko. Facebook and Twitter Q&A. September 21, 2013.

104. Ono, Yoko (@yokoono). Instagram, May 1, 2015.

105. Ono, Yoko. Facebook and Twitter Q&A. May 23, 2014.

106. Hundley, Jessica. "Interview with Artist/Musician Yoko Ono." *Interviews with Icons*, February 9, 2011. https:// interviewswithicons.wordpress.com/2011/02/09/artist musician-yoko-ono/. First published in *Flaunt* magazine.

107. Ono, Yoko, composer/vocalist. "Yes, I'm a Witch." Recorded 1974. Released 1997. Track 6 on *A Story*. Rykodisc, CD. © Ono Music administered by Downtown Music Publishing.

108. Ono, Yoko, composer/vocalist. "Rising." Recorded 1993– 1995. Released November 7, 1995. Track 11 on *Rising*. Capitol / EMI Records, CD. © Ono Music administered by Downtown Music Publishing.

109. Ono, Yoko. *Acorn*. Chapel Hill, NC: Algonquin Books, 2013. © Yoko Ono.

110. Ono, Yoko, composer/vocalist. "What a Bastard the

World Is." Released 1973. Track B5 on *Approximately Infinite Universe*. Apple Records, 2 x vinyl. © Ono Music administered by Downtown Music Publishing.

111. Ono, Yoko, composer/vocalist. "Straight Talk." Released 1973. Track B2 on *Feeling the Space*. Apple Records, vinyl. © Ono Music administered by Downtown Music Publishing.

112. Ono, Yoko, composer/vocalist. "Woman Power." Released 1973. Track B5 on *Feeling the Space*. Apple Records, vinyl. © Ono Music administered by Downtown Music Publishing.

113. Ono, Yoko, composer/vocalist. "Walking on Thin Ice." Released 1981. Side A on *Walking on Thin Ice*. Geffen Records, vinyl, single. © Ono Music administered by Downtown Music Publishing.

114. Ono, Yoko, composer/vocalist. "Dream Love." Released 1982. Track B4 on *It's Alright (I See Rainbows)*. Polydor Records, vinyl. © Ono Music administered by Downtown Music Publishing.

115. Ono, Yoko, composer/vocalist. "Hell in Paradise." Released 1985. Track A1 on *Starpeace*. Polydor Records, vinyl. © Ono Music administered by Downtown Music Publishing.

116. Ono, Yoko, composer/vocalist. "I Love All of Me." Released 1985. Track A2 on *Starpeace*. Polydor Records, vinyl. © Ono Music administered by Downtown Music Publishing.

117. Ono, Yoko, composer/vocalist. "Cape Clear." Released

1985. Track B1 on *Starpeace*. Polydor Records, vinyl. © Ono Music administered by Downtown Music Publishing.

118. Ono, Yoko, composer/vocalist. "It's Gonna Rain (Living on Tiptoe)." Released 1985. Track B4 on *Starpeace*. Polydor Records, vinyl. © Ono Music administered by Downtown Music Publishing.

119. Ono, Yoko, composer/vocalist. "Starpeace." Released 1985. Track B5 on *Starpeace*. Polydor Records, vinyl. © Ono Music administered by Downtown Music Publishing.

120. Ono, Yoko. "Change the Channel." Address presented at Oberlin College, 2010.

121. D'Souza, Shaad. "The World Is Finally Catching Up to Yoko Ono." *Vice*, August 7, 2018. https://www.vice.com/en/article/zmkwkj/yoko-ono-interview-now-or-never-warzone-premiere-watch-listen-2018.

122. D'Arcy, David. "Interview with Yoko Ono: 'I Always Move On.'" *The Art Newspaper*, October 31, 2000. https://www.theartnewspaper.com/2000/11/01/interview-with-yoko-ono-i-always-move-on.

123. Berger, Joshua. "Yoko Ono." *Plazm*, no. 29 (2007): 14–18.

124. Fowler, Justin. "Yoko Ono 'A Stepping Stone to the Future.'" *Volume*, no. 29 (2011).

125. Teeters, Jean. "An Interview with Yoko Ono." *Absolute Elsewhere*. https://articles.absoluteelsewhere.net/Articles/yoko_ono_int.html.

126. Ono, Yoko. Interview by Alexandra Munroe. *New York*.

November 18, 2012. Excerpts first published in *Yoko Ono: Half-a-Wind Show*, edited by Ingrid Pfeiffer and Max Hollein. New York: Prestel, 2013.

127. Robins, Wayne. "Ono Awaits a Brighter Season." *Newsday*, September 13, 1984.

128. Connolly, Ray. *The Evening Standard*, October 26, 1968.

129. Miles. "John Lennon/Yoko Ono Interview." Unpublished, 1969.

130. Alterman, Loraine. "Yoko: How I Rescued John from Chauvinism." *Melody Maker*, September 22, 1973.

131. Edwards, Henry. *Crawdaddy*, August 29, 1971.

132. Needham, Alex. "Yoko Ono: 'To Be an Artist You Need Courage.'" *Guardian*, July 5, 2015. https://www.theguardian.com/environment/2015/jul/05/yoko-ono-to-be-an-artist-you-need-courage.

133. Ono, Yoko. *Shed Light*. 2005.

134. Ono, Yoko (@yokoono). Instagram, June 27, 2017.

IMAGINE PEACE

CHRONOLOGY

1933

Yoko Ono is born on February 18 in Tokyo, Japan.

1936

Ono and her mother travel to San Francisco, where Ono
meets her father for the first time.

1937–1942

The Ono family moves between Japan and New York,
before settling back in Japan, where Ono attends
Keimei Gakuen, a prestigious elementary school.

1945

Ono and her family briefly escape to a bunker in Tokyo.
Then, she and her siblings are evacuated to the
countryside, where they survive the brutal firebomb-
ing of the city by the US Army Air Force on March 9
and 10.

1952

Ono attends Gakushūin University, becoming the first
  female student accepted into the philosophy program.

1953

Ono joins her family in Scarsdale, New York, and enrolls
  at Sarah Lawrence College, which she attends until
  1956.

1956

Ono elopes with the avant-garde composer and pianist
  Toshi Ichiyanagi and moves to Manhattan.

1960

Ono rents a loft at 112 Chambers Street in Lower Manhattan and with La Monte Young begins organizing
  performances and events in the space, becoming a
  vital part of the New York avant-garde.

1961

Ono exhibits her *Instruction Paintings* in her first solo

show. *Paintings and Drawings by Yoko Ono* is presented at George Maciunas' AG Gallery, 925 Madison Avenue, New York.

On November 24, Ono gives a performance of works involving movement, sound, and voice ("Works by Yoko Ono") at the Carnegie Recital Hall in New York.

1962

In March, Ono returns to Tokyo for the first time in nearly ten years for a solo performance and exhibition at Sogetsu Art Center, and remains in Japan for the next two and a half years.

1963

Ono and Ichiyanagi divorce.

Ono meets and marries Anthony Cox. Ono gives birth to their daughter, Kyoko Ono Cox, in Japan.

1964

Ono self-publishes the first edition of *Grapefruit*, her book of instructions for conceptual artworks, in Tokyo.

Ono debuts what is perhaps her best-known artwork, Cut *Piece*, at the Yamaichi Concert Hall in Kyoto, Japan. As later described in the 1970 edition of her book *Grape-fruit*: "It is usually performed by Yoko Ono coming on the stage and, in a sitting position, placing a pair of scissors in front of her and asking the audience to come up on the stage, one by one, and cut a portion of her clothing (anywhere they like) and take it. The performer, however, does not have to be a woman." She goes on to perform the piece in Tokyo, New York, London, and Paris.

Ono returns to New York in September.

1966

Ono makes some of her first films, Film No. 4 ('*Bottoms*'), *Film No. 1* ('*Match*') / *Fluxfilm No. 14*, and *Eyeblink* / *Fluxfilm No. 15*. She also has an exhibition at the Judson Gallery titled *The Stone*, in collaboration with Anthony Cox, Jeffrey Perkins, Michael Mason, and Jon Hendricks.

In September, Ono is invited by Mario Amaya and
Gustav Metzgerto to take part in the *Destruction in Art
Symposium* (DIAS) in London. Ono gives a lecture
and several performances, including *Shadow Piece*, in
a London courtyard. Participants' shadows recall the
victims of the atomic bombs dropped on Hiroshima
and Nagasaki in 1945.

Ono decides to remain in London.

In early November, Ono has a solo exhibition *Unfinished
Paintings & Objects by Yoko Ono* at the Indica Gallery in
London. John Lennon attends before the show opens
to the public, and Ono and Lennon meet for the first
time.

1967

Ono makes a second version of Film No. 4 ('Bottoms')
and stages the *Lion Wrapping Event*, which is also made
into a film.

She opens her solo exhibition *Half-a-Wind Show* at the
Lisson Gallery in London. John Lennon is a guest artist, and it is their first public collaboration as artists.

1968

Ono makes two films with Lennon: *Film No. 5* ('Smile') and *Two Virgins*. Their first collaborative album, *Unfinished Music No. 1: Two Virgins*, is released.

1969

During this year, Lennon and Ono form the Plastic Ono Band, which at this time also features Eric Clapton, Klaus Voormann, and Alan White, though membership to the band will continually shift, by design.

In early February Ono and Cox finalize their divorce.

On March 20, Yoko Ono and John Lennon marry in Gibraltar.

Knowing their marriage would draw attention from the press, in place of a honeymoon, Ono and Lennon perform their weeklong "Bed-in for Peace" in Amsterdam, inviting press into their hotel room daily in an effort to promote world peace. The couple later perform another Bed-in, in Montreal.

In May, Lennon and Ono release the album *Unfinished Music No. 2: Life with the Lions* and the song "The Ballad of John and Yoko."

In July, the Plastic Ono Band releases "Give Peace a
  Chance," which reaches number two on the UK
  charts.

Ono and Lennon release the films *Mr. & Mrs. Lennon's
  Honeymoon*, *Bed Peace*, and "*RAPE*."

In December, Ono and Lennon begin their "WAR IS
  OVER! (If you want it)" campaign with billboards
  across 12 countries, along with newspaper advertise-
  ments and posters.

1970

In February, the Plastic Ono Band releases "Instant
  Karma" (Lennon) and "Who Has Seen the Wind"
  (Ono).

With Lennon, Ono makes four films: *Up Your Legs Forever*,
  Fly, *Freedom*, and *Apotheosis*.

Lennon and Ono begin primal therapy with psycholo-
  gist Arthur Janov.

Simon and Schuster acquires publishing rights and begins to distribute an expanded edition of *Grapefruit*.

In December, Ono releases her debut album, *Yoko Ono/
  Plastic Ono Band*.

1971

Lennon and Ono settle in New York City.

In May, *Apotheosis* and *Fly* are screened at the Cannes Film Festival.

Ono stages a solo conceptual exhibition at the Museum of Modern Art (MoMA) in New York, placing an ad for the unofficial exhibition in the *Village Voice*, without alerting the museum. The project is documented as a film and a catalog is produced, titled *Museum of Modern [F]art*.

On September 20, Ono releases her second studio album, *Fly*.

Ono's solo exhibition *This Is Not Here* opens at the Everson Museum of Art in Syracuse, New York. John Lennon is a guest artist.

1972

Ono and Lennon release the album *Some Time in New York City*, and the film *Imagine*.

Ono participates in *Documenta 5* in Kassel, Germany.

On August 30, Lennon and Ono perform two One to One benefit concerts at Madison Square Garden in

New York. They perform with the band Elephant's
Memory, with guest appearances by Roberta Flack,
Stevie Wonder, Melanie Safka, and Sha Na Na.

1973

Lennon and Ono move to the Dakota, an apartment
building on the Upper West Side in Manhattan.

Ono and Lennon announce the creation of Nutopia, a
conceptual country that has no land, no boundaries,
no passports, only people.

On January 8, Ono releases her third studio album titled
Approximately Infinite Universe.

In September, Ono and Lennon separate. They remain
apart until 1975.

On November 23, Ono releases *Feeling the Space*.

1974

Ono goes on a concert tour in Japan.

1975–79

Ono and Lennon reunite. They remain together until
Lennon's death in 1980.

Ono gives birth to the couple's son, Sean Taro Ono Lennon, on October 9, 1975—John Lennon's thirty-fifth birthday.

1980

In November, Ono and Lennon release *Double Fantasy*. Many of Lennon's songs on the album were written in Bermuda that June, reflecting his newfound stability and family life.

On December 8, Lennon and Ono pose for photographer Annie Leibovitz. During the shoot, Leibovitz captures a fully clothed Ono lying on her back and a naked Lennon embracing Ono in a fetal-like position. The photograph is published as the cover of *Rolling Stone* on January 22, 1981.

That night, John Lennon is fatally shot outside the couple's Manhattan home, the Dakota.

1981

On June 3, Ono releases her fifth studio album, *Season of Glass*, an emotional response to Lennon's death.

1982

Ono and Lennon win the 1981 Grammy Award for Album of the Year for *Double Fantasy* at the twenty-fourth Annual Grammy Awards.

On November 29, Ono releases her sixth studio album, *It's Alright (I See Rainbows)*.

1983

Putnam publishes Ono's book *John Lennon: Summer of 1980*.

1984

Ono releases *Milk and Honey*, a collaborative album with Lennon largely recorded during sessions for *Double Fantasy*.

1985

Starpeace, Ono's seventh studio album, is released on November 29.

Strawberry Fields in Central Park, a memorial dedicated to Lennon, is opened by Ono and her son, Sean, on October 9, the day of Lennon's forty-fifth birthday.

1987

Ono is involved in anti-nuclear activism, attending an international forum in Moscow.

1989

Yoko Ono: Objects, Films opens at the Whitney Museum of American Art in New York. The exhibition of Ono's conceptual objects and *Bronze Age* series is accompanied by a showing of her films. The show signals a renewed interest in Ono's artwork.

1990

Yoko Ono: Objects, Films travels to the Institute of Contemporary Art, Boston.

1992

Ono releases her boxed set *Onobox* with Rykodisc. The collection includes material by Ono dating from 1968 to 1985, presented in six compact discs. The project is produced by Ono.

Random House publishes Ono's book *John Lennon Family Album*.

1993

Kodansha publishes Ono's book *Grapefruit Juice* in Japan.

1994

Ono creates an off-Broadway musical, *New York Rock*, a
    fictionalized account of her and John Lennon's life
    together, with original music by Ono.

1995

Weatherhill publishes Ono's book *Instruction Paintings*.
On November 7, Ono releases *Rising*, her eighth solo
    studio album. The backing band on the album is
    IMA, formed by Sean Lennon.

1997

Yoko Ono: Have You Seen the Horizon Lately? opens at the
    Museum of Modern Art, Oxford. The comprehensive
    exhibition tours to several venues in Europe and
    Israel.
On July 1, *A Story* is released by Rykodisc as a stand-
    alone album. Recorded in 1974, it remained

unreleased until 1992, when portions were included in the boxed set *Onobox*.

1998

Ono's exhibition *Yoko Ono: En Trance—Ex It* is presented in a two-part show at Deitch Projects and the Andre Emmerich Gallery, both in New York. .

2000

On October 18, *YES Yoko Ono*, the first major American retrospective of Ono's work featuring approximately 150 works from 1960 to 2000, opens at the Japan Society Gallery in New York. Curated by Alexandra Munroe with Jon Hendricks, it travels to twelve additional venues. The exhibition is accompanied by the book *YES Yoko Ono*, published by Harry N. Abrams.

2001

On November 9, Ono releases *Blueprint for a Sunrise*, her tenth studio album.

2002

Ono establishes the LennonOno Grant for Peace.

2003

Ono's exhibition *Odyssey of a Cockroach* opens at Deitch
   Projects in New York. A catalog is produced to
   accompany the show.

Ono's work is shown at the fiftieth Venice Biennale in
   Utopia Station.

Ono performs *Cut Piece* at the Theatre le Ranelagh in Paris
   for the first time since the 1960s, in conjunction
   with her exhibition *Yoko Ono: Women's Room* at Musée
   d'Art Moderne de Paris.

2005

Horizontal Memories opens at the Astrup Fearnley Museum
   of Modern Art in Oslo, and tours to venues in
   Switzerland and Brazil.

Ono's edited collection, *Memories of John Lennon*, is
   published by HarperCollins.

2007

Ono's IMAGINE PEACE TOWER is unveiled on Viðey Island, off the coast of Reykjavík, Iceland, on Lennon's birthday, October 9. The work is dedicated to John Lennon and symbolizes their continuing work toward world peace. An annual lighting ceremony occurs each year on October 9.

2009

Between My Head and the Sky, Ono's eleventh studio album, is released by Chimera Music on September 21. The album is coproduced by Ono and Sean Lennon.

Between the Sky and My Head opens at Kunsthalle Bielefeld in Germany and travels to Baltic Centre for Contemporary Art in Gateshead Newcastle, UK.

Ono is awarded the Golden Lion for Lifetime Achievement at the fifty-third Venice Biennale and has a solo exhibition, *Anton's Memory*, at the same time in Venice. Ono's *The Other Rooms* is published in conjunction with the exhibition.

Ono establishes the Courage Awards for the Arts.

2010

MoMA installs an Ono *Wish Tree* in its sculpture garden
as part of the exhibition *Contemporary Art from the Collection.* Other works by Ono are also shown, including
Museum of Modern [F]art.

2011

Ono is awarded the eighth Hiroshima Art Prize, recog-
nizing artists' contributions to peace, which includes
a major exhibition of her work at the Hiroshima
Museum of Contemporary Art.

2012

Ono and her son Sean form the group Artists Against
Fracking, successfully campaigning to ban fracking
in New York State.
Yoko Ono: To the Light opens at Serpentine Gallery, London.

2013

In July, Ono publishes *Acorn* with OR Books. The
collection of instructions was originally published
in installments as an online project in 1996–97.

Yoko Ono: Half-a-Wind Show opens at the Schirn Kunsthalle in Frankfurt, Germany. The major survey exhibition tours four venues in Europe, including the Louisiana Museum in Denmark and the Guggenheim Bilbao.

On September 17, Chimera Music releases Ono's twelfth studio album, *Take Me to the Land of Hell*. The album is coproduced by Ono, Sean Lennon, and Yuka C. Honda.

2015

Yoko Ono: One Woman Show, 1960–71 opens at MoMA in New York.

Yoko Ono: From My Window opens at the Museum of Contemporary Art in Tokyo.

2016

In October, *SKYLANDING* is unveiled in Chicago's Jackson Park. The sculpture is a permanent public installation.

Yoko Ono: Lumière de L'Aube opens at MAC Lyon in France.

2018

Thames and Hudson releases Ono's book *Imagine John Yoko*.

Ono releases her thirteenth studio album, *Warzone*, on October 24.

SKY, a permanent installation of six mosaic murals, is unveiled at the MTA - 72nd Street Subway Station, steps away from Ono's home at the Dakota.

2019

Yoko Ono: PEACE Is POWER, a site-specific installation commissioned by MoMA in New York, opens and is on view for three years.

Growing Freedom: The Instructions of Yoko Ono and the Art of John and Yoko opens at the PHI Foundation for Contemporary Art in Montreal, Canada. The exhibition travels to two additional venues in Canada, including Vancouver Art Gallery.

Yoko Ono: PEACE Is POWER opens at Museum der bildenden Kunste in Leipzig, Germany.

2020

Yoko Ono: The Learning Garden of Freedom opens at Serralves
   Museum of Contemporary Art in Porto, Portugal.

2022

Yoko Ono: This Room Moves at the Same Speed as the Clouds
   opens at Kunsthaus Zürich in Switzerland.

2023

Yoko Ono—PEACE Is POWER opens at the Nobel Peace
   Center in Oslo, Norway. It is the institution's first
   exhibition dedicated to an artist's work.
On February 18, Ono celebrates her ninetieth birthday.

2024

Yoko Ono: Music of the Mind opens at Tate Modern, London.

ACKNOWLEDGMENTS

First and foremost, my profound thanks go to Yoko Ono, whose unparalleled voice and mind comprise the quotes in this book. I am honored to be aligned with such a deep thinker and revolutionary spirit. Your creativity and insights are an inspiration to us all.

My heartfelt thanks as well to Sean Taro Ono Lennon, who made this book possible. My deepest thanks as well to the teams at Herbsman, Hafer, Weber & Frisch LLP and Epic Rights for their support and presence throughout this project. Special thanks goes to Jonas Herbsman, Dorothy Weber, Connor Monahan, Simon Hilton, Sam Gannon, Grace Davyd, Lisa Streff, and Jessica Pearson. Thanks as well to Ashley Rodriguez, Eric Montemayor, Jordan Meltzer, Andrianna Caban, and Ashley Fogerty.

I would also like to thank Paul Schindler for his guidance on this and many other projects

My sincere appreciation to the entire team at Princeton University Press, especially Michelle Komie, Christie Henry, Terri O'Prey, Cathy Slovensky Colleen Suljic, Laurie

Schlesinger, Cathy Felgar, Jodi Price, Kathryn Stevens, Annie Miller, and Mark Bellis. We remain extremely grateful to PUP for their continued professionalism, encouragement, and passion for our projects together throughout the years.

I would also like to acknowledge Lenny McGurr, Brian Donnelly, Andy Cohen, John Pelosi, Angelo DiStefano, Mike Dean, and Louise Donegan.

Very special thanks to Editorial Director Fiona Graham for her invaluable research and organization of this publication.

My sincere thanks to Taliesin Thomas for her amazing assistance on this project and many others, and to Steven Rodríguez for his continued support.

My thanks as well to Matthew Christensen and Susan Delson for their editorial assistance.

Finally, I give all my bottomless gratitude to my amazing wife, Abbey, and to my wonderful children, Justin, Ethan, Ellie, and Jonah for their love and encouragement.

As always, I give endless love and thanks to my mother Judith.

LARRY WARSH

ILLUSTRATIONS

Frontispiece: Portrait of Yoko Ono. Photo by Iain Macmillan. © Yoko Ono Lennon.

Page 122: Yoko Ono, IMAGINE PEACE 2022.

Yoko Ono was born in Tokyo, Japan, and moved to New York in the early 1950s. Heavily involved in the Conceptual and Fluxus art movements, her early works were often based on instructions communicated verbally or in written form, such as her groundbreaking artist's book *Grapefruit* (1964). Her career in fine art also includes revolutionary works of performance art, installations, and film, and her performance piece *Cut Piece* (1964) is regarded as a landmark of performance and feminist art. Her work has been the subject of numerous exhibitions and retrospectives in major international museums, including Tate Modern, the Museum of Modern Art in New York, the Japan Society of New York, the Kunsthaus Zürich, and the Guggenheim Museum Bilbao, among others. Ono was also the co-founder of the Plastic Ono Band with her late husband, John Lennon, and has written and performed thirteen solo albums throughout her career. A dedicated social activist, Ono has been at the forefront of the peace movement and continues to stage global interventions to this day.

Larry Warsh has been active in the art world for over thirty years as a publisher and artist-collaborator. An early collector of Keith Haring and Jean-Michel Basquiat, Warsh was a lead organizer for the exhibition *Basquiat: The Unknown Notebooks*, which debuted at the Brooklyn Museum, NY in 2015 and continues to travel to international museums. He has loaned artworks by Haring and Basquiat from his collection to numerous exhibitions worldwide, and he served as a curatorial consultant on *Keith Haring | Jean-Michel Basquiat: Crossing Lines* for the National Gallery of Victoria, Melbourne. The founder of *Museums Magazine*, Warsh has been involved in numerous publishing projects and is the editor of several titles published by Princeton University Press, including *Basquiat-isms* (2019), *Haring-isms* (2020), *Futura-isms* (2021), *Abloh-isms* (2021), *Arsham-isms* (2021), *Warhol-isms* (2022), *Hirst-isms* (2022), *Jean-Michel Basquiat: The Notebooks* (2017), *Keith Haring: 31 Subway Drawings* (2021), *Daniel Arsham: Sketchbook* (2022), and two books by Ai Weiwei, *Humanity* (2018) and *Weiwei-isms* (2012). Warsh has served on the board of the Getty Museum Photographs Council and was a founding member of the Basquiat Authentication Committee from 1993 until its dissolution in 2012.

ISMs

Larry Warsh, Series Editor

The ISMs series distills the voices of an exciting range of visual artists and designers into captivating, beautifully made books of quotations for a new generation of readers. In turn passionate, inspiring, humorous, witty, and challenging, these collections offer powerful statements on topics ranging from contemporary culture, politics, and race, to creativity, humanity, and the role of art in the world. Books in this series are edited by Larry Warsh and published by Princeton University Press in association with No More Rulers.

Obrist-isms, Hans Ulrich Obrist

Calder-isms, Alexander Calder

Ono-isms, Yoko Ono

Minter-isms, Marilyn Minter

Fairey-isms, Shepard Fairey

JR-isms, JR

Abramović-isms, Marina Abramović